ANCIENT EGYPT FOR KIDS

CAROLYN DICKSON

ANCIENT EGYPT FOR KIDS: *Explore the Nile, Meet the Pharaohs, and Unlock the Secrets of the Pyramids*

Copyright © 2025 by Dylanna Publishing, Inc.

Disclaimer: This book is intended for educational and entertainment purposes. While every effort has been made to ensure historical accuracy, our understanding of ancient civilizations continues to evolve as new archaeological discoveries are made. Some historical details may be interpreted differently by various scholars. This book presents information that is widely accepted by historians and archaeologists as of the publication date.

ISBN: 978-1-64790-441-8 (paperback)
ISBN: 978-1-64790-477-7 (hardcover)
Publisher: Dylanna Publishing, Inc.
First Edition: 2025

10 9 8 7 6 5 4 3 2 1

Publisher's Cataloging-in-Publication Data

Names: Dickson, Carolyn, author.
Title: Ancient Egypt for kids : explore the Nile, meet the
pharaohs, and unlock the secrets of the pyramids / Carolyn
Dickson.
Description: West Barnstable, MA : Dylanna Publishing, Inc.,
2025 | Series: History explorers | Audience: Ages 8-12.
Identifiers: ISBN 978-1-64790-441-8 (paperback)
Subjects: LCSH: Egypt--History--To 332 B.C.--Juvenile literature. |
Egypt--Civilization--To 332 B.C.--Juvenile literature. | Egypt--
Social life and customs--To 332 B.C.--Juvenile literature.
Classification: LCC DT61 .D53 2025 | DDC 932--dc23

For information about special discounts for bulk purchases, please contact:
orders@dylannapublishing.com
Dylanna Publishing, Inc.
www.dylannapublishing.com

Contents

Introduction

Get ready to step back in time over 4,000 years to one of the most amazing civilizations the world has ever seen. In this book, you'll discover how the mighty Nile River created an entire civilization in the middle of the desert. You'll meet powerful pharaohs who built monuments that have lasted thousands of years, and learn about ordinary Egyptian families who lived, worked, and played along the riverbanks.

You'll explore massive pyramids and mysterious tombs, decode hieroglyphic writing that looks like picture puzzles, and uncover some of the strangest (and funniest!) facts about ancient Egyptian life.

You'll meet the real people behind these incredible achievements. There's the brilliant architect who became a god, the brave soldier who saved a pharaoh's life, and the powerful queens who ruled empires. You'll also discover what life was like for kids just like you who played games and went to school (well, some of them did!).

Ancient Egypt lasted for over 3,000 years. That's longer than any civilization in history. By the time you finish this book, you'll understand why this remarkable place continues to capture our imagination and teach us what humans can accomplish when they dream big and work together.

So grab your explorer's hat and get ready for an adventure. You'll sail down the Nile, go inside the Great Pyramid, and come face-to-face with mummies and pharaohs.

Ancient Egypt is waiting. Let's go discover its secrets!

MEDITERRANEAN SEA
Jerusalem
Rosetta
Damietta
Gaza
Alexandria
Buto
Rafah
Sais
Tanis
Pelusium
Naukratis
Busiris
Avaris
LOWER EGYPT
Bubastis
Merimda
Canal Bitter Lake
Negev
Heliopolis
Giza
Cairo
Sinai
Saqqara
Memphis
Dahshur
Helwan
Timna
Lake Moeris
Fayum Oasis
Meydum
Lahun
Serabit el-Khadim
Herakleopolis
Gulf of Suez
Gulf of Aqaba
Bahariya Oasis
Nile River
Beni Hasan
Hermopolis
Amarna
Red Sea
Qis
Western Desert
Asyut
Badari
UPPER EGYPT
Qau
Akhmim
Eastern Desert
Thinis
Nile River
Abydos
Dendera
Quseir
Naqada
Kopos
Khorga Oasis
Thebes
(Luxor, Karnak)
Dakhla Oasis
Tod
Hierakonpolis
Edfu
Kom Ombo
Elephantine
Aswan
First Cataract
Dunqul Oasis
Toshka Lakes
Lake Nasser
Nabta Playa
Abu Simbel
Buhen
Ikon
Second Cataract
(Great Cataract)
NUBIA
Nubian Desert

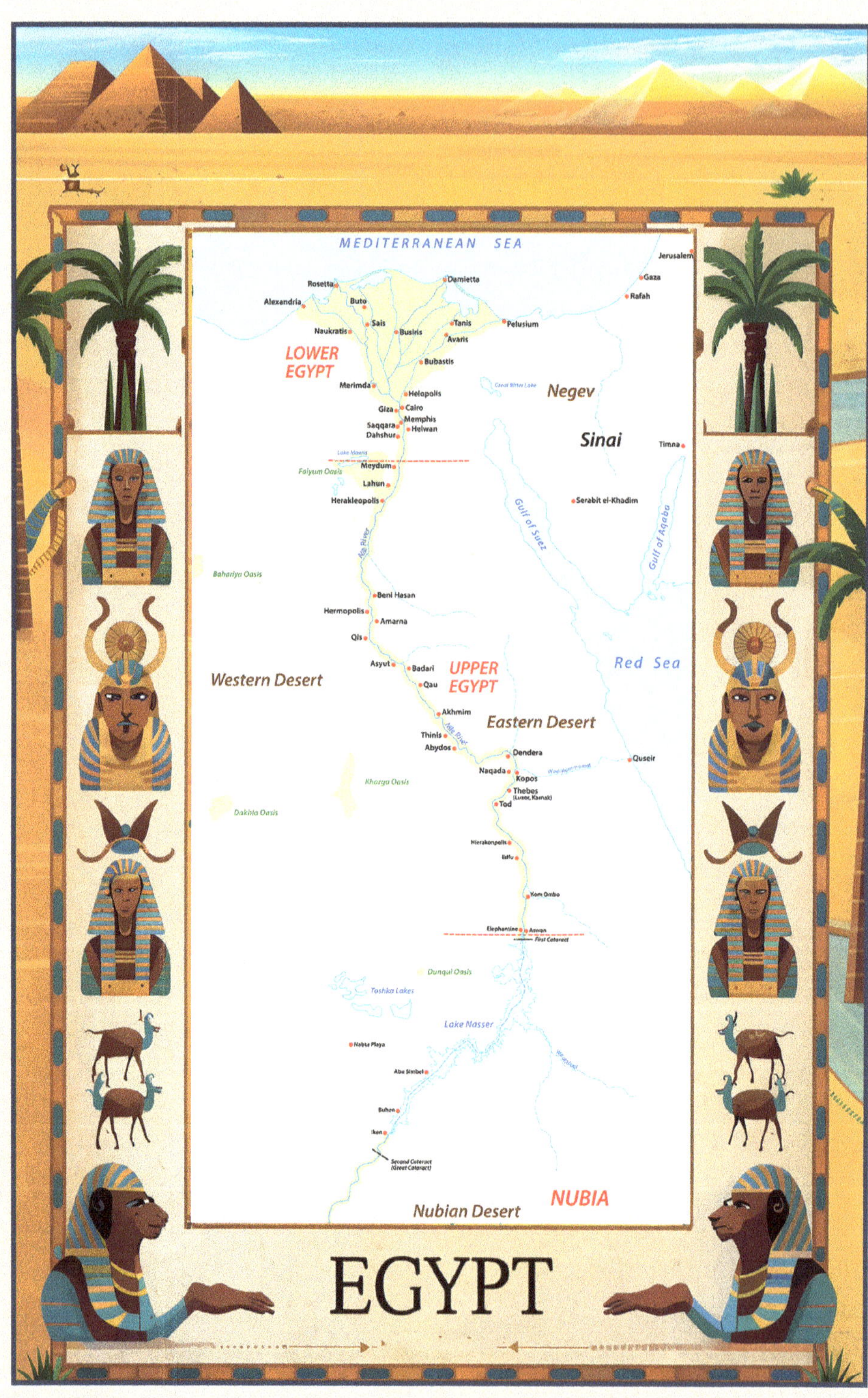

EGYPT

Chapter 1
What Was Ancient Egypt?

Picture a place where kings were considered gods on Earth, where massive stone pyramids reached toward the sky, and where people believed so strongly in life after death that they spent decades preparing for it. Welcome to Ancient Egypt—one of the most fascinating civilizations that ever existed!

For over 3,000 years, ancient Egyptians created art, built monuments, and developed ideas that still amaze us today. While most of Europe was just figuring out how to farm, Egyptians were performing surgery, creating detailed calendars, and building structures so incredible that people still can't agree on exactly how they did it.

When and Where Was Ancient Egypt?

Ancient Egypt lasted longer than almost any civilization in history—over 3,000 years, from around 3100 BCE to 30 BCE. To put that in perspective, the Roman Empire lasted about 1,000 years and the United States has been around for less than 250 years. That means ancient Egypt thrived for more than three times longer than the Romans and twelve times longer than the U.S. has existed.

This incredible civilization grew up along the banks of the Nile River in northeastern Africa, in the same place where modern Egypt exists today. The country was about the size of Texas and California combined, but most people lived in a narrow strip of green land along the river—only about 10 miles wide but stretching for hundreds of miles.

The ancient Egyptians called their land "Kemet," which means "black land," because of the rich, dark soil left behind by the Nile's yearly floods. They called the surrounding desert "Deshret," meaning "red land." This black land versus red land distinction was crucial—the black land meant life and prosperity, while the red land meant death and danger.

The Mighty Nile: Egypt's Lifeline

If you wanted to understand Ancient Egypt in one word, that word would be "Nile." This amazing river was everything to the ancient Egyptians—their highway, their calendar, their source of life, and their gift from the gods.

The Nile is the longest river in the world, stretching over 4,000 miles from central Africa to the Mediterranean Sea. But for the ancient Egyptians, the most important part was the section that flowed through their land, bringing life to what would otherwise have been empty desert.

Every year, like clockwork, the Nile would flood between July and October. This wasn't a disaster—it was the most wonderful time of year! The flooding deposited rich, fertile soil along the riverbanks, creating perfect farmland in the middle of the desert. Without this yearly miracle, Egypt would have been just another patch of sand. With it, Egypt became the breadbasket of the ancient world.

Why Ancient Egypt Captures Our Imagination

You've probably seen pictures of pyramids, mummies, and pharaohs in movies or museums. But why does Ancient Egypt fascinate us more than almost any other ancient civilization?

They built some of humanity's greatest monuments. The Great Pyramid of Giza was the tallest building in the world for nearly 4,000 years! Even today, with all our modern technology, archaeologists are still impressed by how precisely they built it.

They mastered preservation like no one else. Thanks to mummification and Egypt's dry climate, we can literally look ancient pharaohs in the face in museums around the world. King Tutankhamun died over 3,300 years ago, but his mummy is so well-preserved that scientists can tell what he ate for his last meal!

They created beautiful, mysterious writing. Egyptian hieroglyphs look like a puzzle made of pictures—birds, eyes, water ripples, and human figures all mixed together. Each symbol could represent a sound, a word, or an idea.

They were incredibly advanced for their time. Ancient Egyptians performed surgery, created a 365-day calendar almost identical to ours, made paper from plants, and invented many things we still use today. They even had toothpaste and breath mints!

Their stories seem almost too incredible to be true. From boy kings who ruled empires to powerful queens who wore fake beards, from cursed tombs to cat goddesses, Ancient Egypt is packed with tales that sound like fantasy movies—except they really happened.

A Civilization That Changed the World

Ancient Egypt wasn't just an old civilization that built some cool monuments. The Egyptians were inventors, artists, doctors, and engineers who created innovations we still use today.

They gave us the 24-hour day, developed some of the world's first organized medicine, and created beautiful art that influenced Greek and Roman civilizations. Most importantly, they showed us that humans can achieve incredible things when they work together toward a common goal.

Whether they were building a pyramid that would last forever or developing new ways to help sick people get better, the ancient Egyptians believed in doing things that mattered and would outlast their own lives.

Meeting the Real Ancient Egyptians

Thanks to hieroglyphic writing, tomb paintings, and well-preserved artifacts, we can get to know ancient Egyptians almost like neighbors. We can read their letters, see

Old Kingdom
(c. 2686–2181 BCE)
The Age of the Pyramids. Pharaohs built massive tombs like the Great Pyramid of Giza to last forever.

Middle Kingdom
(c. 2055–1650 BCE)
A time of rebuilding and unity. Art, writing, and trade flourished across Egypt.

New Kingdom
(c. 1550–1070 BCE)
Egypt's golden age of power. Great pharaohs like Hatshepsut and Ramses II ruled a mighty empire.

Cleopatra's Reign
(51–30 BCE)
The last pharaoh of Egypt, Cleopatra tried to save Egypt as Rome rose to power.

paintings of their pets, and find out what they liked to eat
and how they spent their free time.

In this book, you'll meet fascinating people like Hatshepsut, a
woman who became pharaoh and wore a fake beard to show her
authority, and Imhotep, a brilliant architect who was so respected
that people worshipped him as a god. You'll discover what it was
like to be a kid in ancient Egypt and learn about their strange but
effective medical treatments.

Did You Know?

Egypt is one of the oldest civilizations in the world!
While Ancient Egypt was building pyramids around 2500
BCE, most of Europe was still in the Stone Age. The ancient Egyptians were performing surgery, making paper,
and creating detailed calendars while many other parts
of the world were just learning to farm!

As we explore Ancient Egypt together, you'll discover how the
Nile River shaped everything about Egyptian life, meet the god-
kings called pharaohs, learn about their fascinating beliefs about
death and the afterlife, and uncover secrets that archaeologists
are still discovering today.

Get ready for an adventure that spans thousands of years and will
show you how amazing human civilization can be when people
dare to dream big and work together.

Welcome to Ancient Egypt—prepare to be amazed!

Chapter 2

The River That Made Egypt

Imagine standing in a burning desert where nothing grows for hundreds of miles. The sun beats down mercilessly, there's no water anywhere, and you can't see a single tree or blade of grass. Now imagine that just a few miles away, there's a sparkling blue river surrounded by green fields, palm trees, and bustling cities.

This incredible contrast is exactly what made the Nile River so special—and why Ancient Egypt became one of the world's greatest civilizations. Without the Nile River, there would be no Ancient Egypt. It's that simple.

The World's Greatest River

The Nile River isn't just long—it's the longest river on Earth, winding 4,132 miles from the mountains of East Africa to the Mediterranean Sea. That's like a river flowing from New York City to Los Angeles and then halfway back again!

But length wasn't what made the Nile magical. What made it incredible was what it did every single year, as predictable as your birthday. While rivers in other parts of the world might flood randomly or not at all, the Nile followed a perfect schedule that Egyptians could count on.

Every summer, heavy rains in Ethiopia sent massive amounts of water rushing down the Nile. By July, the river would swell. By August, it would overflow its banks and flood the entire Nile Valley. Instead of being a disaster, this was the most wonderful time of year—ancient Egyptians called it "Akhet," or the "season of flooding."

The Gift That Kept on Giving

When the floodwaters went down in October, they left behind something more precious than gold: a thick layer of rich, black soil called silt. This soil was so fertile that farmers could grow almost anything in it. Wheat, barley, vegetables, and fruit trees all thrived in this magical dirt that the Nile delivered for free every year.

The ancient Egyptians were so grateful that they created their entire calendar around the Nile's rhythm. Their year had three seasons: Akhet (flooding), Peret (growing), and Shemu (harvesting). Everything in Egyptian life—from religious festivals to work schedules—revolved around what the Nile was doing.

A Greek historian named Herodotus once called Egypt "the gift of the Nile," and he was absolutely right. Take away the Nile, and Egypt would be nothing but empty desert. With the Nile, Egypt became the breadbasket of the ancient world.

Egypt's Ancient Highway

The Nile wasn't just about farming—it was also Ancient Egypt's main highway. In a time before cars, trains, or paved roads, the Nile provided a smooth, fast way to travel and transport goods across the entire country.

Egyptian boats had a clever system that used both the river's current and the wind. When they wanted to go north (downstream toward the Mediterranean), they let the current carry them. When they needed to go south (upstream), they raised their sails and let the wind push them. The wind in Egypt almost always blows from north to south, so it was like having a two-way highway powered by nature!

Traders used the Nile to carry everything from grain and gold to exotic animals and precious stones. Messages from the pharaoh could travel from one end of Egypt to the other. Massive blocks of stone for pyramids and temples floated down the river on barges—some of these stones weighed as much as 30 cars, but they moved easily on the water.

Life Along the Banks

Ancient Egyptians were so dependent on the Nile that virtually everyone lived within a few miles of its banks. If you could fly over Ancient Egypt, it would look like a long, green snake winding through an ocean of yellow sand.

Farmers built an amazing system of canals and irrigation channels to control the Nile's water. They invented clever devices like the shaduf—a long pole with a bucket on one end and a weight on the other—to lift water from the

river to their fields. Some of these ancient systems worked so well that farmers in Egypt still use similar methods today!

Fishing was another huge part of life along the Nile. The river teemed with dozens of different types of fish, and Egyptian artists loved painting scenes of fishermen casting nets from small papyrus boats. Fish was such an important food that some types were considered sacred in certain parts of Egypt.

The River's Amazing Gifts

The Nile provided much more than water and fish. The marshes along the river grew papyrus—a tall, reed-like plant that Egyptians turned into an early form of paper. They also used papyrus to make boats, baskets, sandals, and rope. Basically, papyrus was like the ancient Egyptian version of plastic—they made everything out of it!

The Nile's yearly cycle also gave Egyptians something many other civilizations lacked: predictability. Farmers could plan their entire year around the Nile's reliable schedule. This allowed Egyptian civilization to develop art, science, and architecture because people didn't have to spend all their time worrying about survival.

A River of Gods

To the ancient Egyptians, the Nile wasn't just a river—it was a god. They worshipped Hapi, the god of the annual flood, who was often depicted as a large, friendly man with blue-green skin and a crown made of papyrus plants. If they kept Hapi happy, he would bring a good flood. If they made him angry, the flood might be too small (causing famine) or too large (destroying homes).

The Egyptians also believed that after death, they would sail across a heavenly version of the Nile with Ra, the sun god. Even in their vision of the afterlife, the Nile remained central to everything.

How did rivers shape other civilizations too?

Egypt wasn't the only great civilization built around a river:

- **Mesopotamia**—Built between the Tigris and Euphrates rivers
- **Ancient China**—Grew along the Yellow and Yangtze rivers
- **Indus Valley**—Flourished along the Indus River

Rivers provided water, transportation, fertile soil, and fish everywhere—that's why many of the world's oldest cities are still on riverbanks today!

The Nile River was more than just water flowing through the desert—it was the beating heart of Ancient Egypt. Every aspect of Egyptian life flowed from this incredible river. The ancient Egyptians understood that humans and nature are connected, and they learned to work with the Nile rather than fight it.

Understanding the Nile helps us understand why Ancient Egypt lasted for over 3,000 years. When you have a reliable source of water, food, and transportation, you can focus on building something that lasts. And the ancient Egyptians definitely built things that lasted!

Next, we'll meet the incredible rulers who controlled this river kingdom—the god-kings called pharaohs...

Chapter 3
Pharaohs: Egypt's God-Kings

Imagine being so powerful that millions of people believed you were literally a god walking on Earth. Imagine owning everything in an entire country and having armies who would die to protect you. Imagine people building massive stone monuments just to make sure you had a nice place to spend eternity.

That was the life of an Egyptian pharaoh—the most powerful rulers the ancient world had ever seen. For over 3,000 years, these god-kings shaped one of history's greatest civilizations.

More Than Just Kings

The word "pharaoh" means "great house" in ancient Egyptian, referring to the palace where the ruler lived. But calling a pharaoh just a "king" would be like calling a hurricane just "some wind." Pharaohs were in a completely different category.

Ancient Egyptians believed their pharaoh was the living form of Horus, the falcon-headed god of the sky. When a pharaoh died, they joined with Osiris, the god of the underworld. This wasn't just a nice story—Egyptians literally believed their ruler was divine.

This god-like status gave pharaohs incredible power. Their word was law because questioning a pharaoh meant questioning the gods themselves. When a pharaoh said "build a pyramid," people didn't ask "why?" They asked "how big?" and "when do we start?"

But being a pharaoh wasn't all golden crowns and absolute power. Pharaohs were expected to keep the gods happy, ensure the Nile flooded properly, protect Egypt from enemies, and maintain order. If things went wrong, it was the pharaoh's fault.

The Crown and the Symbols

Pharaohs had special symbols that showed their divine power. The most famous was the double crown—a combination of the white crown of Upper Egypt and the red crown of Lower Egypt. Wearing this showed the pharaoh ruled the entire unified kingdom.

Pharaohs also carried a crook and flail, symbols borrowed from Osiris. The crook showed the pharaoh's role as protector of the Egyptian people, while the flail represented their power to punish enemies.

Most famous was the uraeus—a cobra symbol worn on the pharaoh's forehead. According to legend, this cobra would spit fire at anyone who threatened the pharaoh. Many pharaohs also wore a false beard made of gold, another symbol connecting them to the gods.

Tutankhamun: The Boy King Mystery

One of the most famous pharaohs was also one of the youngest and most mysterious. Tutankhamun became pharaoh when he was only about nine years old—imagine being in fourth grade and suddenly ruling an entire country! He died at eighteen or nineteen, probably never getting the chance to grow into his power.

King Tut would have been forgotten except for one amazing fact: his tomb was found almost completely intact in 1922. While tomb robbers had looted most pharaohs' burials, Tut's tomb was hidden and mostly left undisturbed.

What archaeologist Howard Carter found was mind-blowing: over 5,000 precious objects, including Tut's famous golden burial mask (which weighs 24 pounds of solid gold), chariots, jewelry, weapons, and even board games for the afterlife.

But Tut's story is also tragic. When scientists examined his mummy, they discovered he had a clubfoot, broken ribs, and a fractured skull. Some think he died in a chariot accident, others believe he was murdered. The mystery continues today, making Tutankhamun one of history's most intriguing rulers.

Khufu: Builder of the Great Pyramid

While Tutankhamun is famous for his tomb, Pharaoh Khufu is famous for building the most incredible monument in human history—the Great Pyramid of Giza. Ruling around 2580 BCE, Khufu decided he wanted a tomb that would amaze the world forever. He got his wish.

Khufu was an ambitious ruler who thought big. Building his pyramid wasn't just about creating a tomb—it was about showing the world Egypt's power and his own divine authority. The project required him to organize the largest construction workforce in human history, with estimates suggesting 20,000 workers labored on his pyramid during flood season each year.

The pharaoh personally oversaw many aspects of the construction. Ancient records show that Khufu was deeply involved in the pyramid's design, working closely with his architects to ensure every detail met his exacting standards. He demanded perfection, and his workers delivered it—the pyramid's base is so precisely square that the difference between its longest and shortest sides is only 2 centimeters.

Khufu's pyramid broke every record of its time. At 481 feet tall, it was nearly twice the height of any structure ever built before. It remained the world's tallest building for almost 4,000 years—longer than any skyscraper has held that record. The pharaoh had created something that would outlast every empire that came after him.

Ironically, we know very little about Khufu as a person. He spent 20 years and employed thousands of workers to build his eternal monument, but grave robbers looted his burial chamber thousands of years ago. The man who built the world's most famous tomb became a mystery himself.

Akhenaten: The Revolutionary Pharaoh

Around 1353 BCE, a pharaoh came to power who would turn Egyptian religion and society upside down. Amenhotep IV, who later changed his name to Akhenaten, made a shocking decision: Egypt's hundreds of traditional gods were wrong. There was only one true god—the sun disk called Aten.

This was revolutionary. For over 1,000 years, Egyptians had worshipped many gods with powerful priests managing elaborate temples. Akhenaten declared all of this false and ordered that only Aten be worshipped. He closed temples, fired priests, and moved Egypt's capital from Thebes to a brand-new city he built in the desert.

Akhenaten also revolutionized Egyptian art. Instead of the formal, idealized style used for centuries, artists began creating more realistic, emotional representations. Paintings from his reign show the royal family in intimate moments—playing with children and displaying genuine affection.

But Akhenaten's revolution was too radical for Egypt. After his death, his son Tutankhamun restored the traditional gods and abandoned the new capital. Later pharaohs tried to erase Akhenaten from history, calling him "the heretic" and destroying his monuments.

Ramses II: The Great Show-Off

If you wanted to meet an ancient Egyptian with a massive ego, Ramses II would be your pharaoh. Ruling for an incredible 66 years (1279-1213 BCE), Ramses had plenty of time to cover Egypt with monuments celebrating his own greatness—and he took full advantage.

The temple at Abu Simbel features four colossal statues of Ramses, each 65 feet tall—about as high as a six-story building. He also had

a habit of carving his name over other pharaohs' monuments, basically ancient Egyptian graffiti on a royal scale.

But Ramses wasn't just about bragging. He was a skilled military commander who fought the famous Battle of Kadesh against the Hittite Empire and eventually signed one of history's first peace treaties. Ramses lived to the incredible age of 90 and had over 100 children with his many wives.

Even in death, Ramses got what he wanted: people are still talking about him over 3,000 years later!

Thutmose III: Egypt's Greatest Warrior

While some pharaohs built monuments and others changed  religion, Thutmose III built an empire. Ruling from 1479 to 1425 BCE, he fought 17 military campaigns and never lost a single battle, earning him the nickname "Egypt's Napoleon."

Thutmose III expanded Egypt's borders farther than any pharaoh before or after him. His armies marched into Nubia, Syria, and Palestine, bringing back incredible wealth in tribute. He was also a brilliant strategist who used new military technologies like horse-drawn chariots and composite bows.

But Thutmose III was more than just a warrior. He was also a great builder who constructed temples throughout Egypt and established trade networks that brought exotic goods from across the known world. Under his rule, Egypt became the richest and most powerful nation on Earth.

Timeline: The God-Kings
- **Khufu** (c. 2589-2566 BCE)—Built the Great Pyramid of Giza
- **Thutmose III** (c. 1479-1425 BCE)—Egypt's greatest military pharaoh
- **Akhenaten** (c. 1353-1336 BCE)—Revolutionary who changed Egypt's religion
- **Tutankhamun** (c. 1332-1323 BCE)—The mysterious boy king
- **Ramses II** (c. 1279-1213 BCE)—The great boaster who ruled for 66 years

---

For over 3,000 years, pharaohs ruled Egypt as living gods, each leaving their own unique mark on history. Some built incredible monuments, others conquered vast territories, and a few tried to change Egyptian society completely. But all shared one trait: they believed they were divine beings whose actions would echo through eternity.

These god-kings created a civilization so impressive that we're still amazed by their achievements thousands of years later. But Egypt's story isn't complete without the remarkable women who also wielded pharaonic power—queens and female pharaohs who proved that divine authority wasn't limited to men.

Next, we'll meet the extraordinary women who ruled Egypt and shaped its destiny...

CHAPTER 4
Egypt's Powerful Women

In most ancient civilizations, women had very little power. They couldn't own property, couldn't rule kingdoms, and were expected to stay quietly in the background while men made all the important decisions. But ancient Egypt was different. Egyptian women enjoyed more rights and freedoms than women almost anywhere else in the ancient world—and some of the most fascinating pharaohs and queens in Egyptian history were women.

These weren't just pretty faces sitting beside powerful husbands. These were brilliant, ambitious, and sometimes ruthless rulers who commanded armies, built monuments, and shaped the destiny of one of history's greatest civilizations.

Hatshepsut: The Woman Who Became Pharaoh

The most remarkable female pharaoh was Hatshepsut, who came to power around 1479 BCE in a way that would challenge anyone. When her husband Pharaoh Thutmose II died after only a few years of rule, he left behind a young son from another wife. Hatshepsut was supposed to serve as regent until the boy was old enough to rule, but she had much bigger plans.

Within a few years, Hatshepsut declared herself pharaoh—not just queen, but full pharaoh with all the divine authority that title carried. This was almost unheard of in ancient Egypt. To legitimize her rule in a society that expected pharaohs to be male, she had to be incredibly clever.

Hatshepsut often had herself depicted wearing the traditional false beard of the pharaohs and dressed in men's royal clothing in official art and statues. But don't think she was just pretending to be a man—Hatshepsut was proving that leadership had nothing to do with gender and everything to do with skill.

Her reign was one of the most successful in Egyptian history. Instead of focusing on wars and conquests like many pharaohs, Hatshepsut concentrated on trade, building projects, and making Egypt wealthy and prosperous. She organized famous expeditions to the mysterious land of Punt (probably modern-day Somalia) that brought back gold, ivory, exotic animals, and fragrant incense trees.

Hatshepsut also commissioned some of Egypt's most beautiful architecture. Her mortuary temple at Deir el-Bahari, with its elegant terraces carved directly into the cliffs, is still considered one of the masterpieces of ancient architecture.

For many years after her death, later pharaohs tried to erase Hatshepsut from history by destroying her statues and chiseling her name off monuments. They couldn't stand the idea that a woman had been such a successful pharaoh. But enough evidence survived to reveal her as one of Egypt's greatest rulers, proving that female leadership could be just as effective as male rule.

Cleopatra VII: The Last Pharaoh

When most people hear "Cleopatra," they think of a beautiful Egyptian queen with dramatic eye makeup who had romantic relationships with Julius Caesar and Mark Antony. But the real Cleopatra was far more interesting than any Hollywood movie could capture—she was brilliant, ambitious, spoke nine languages fluently, and was one of the most politically smart rulers in ancient history.

Cleopatra VII was born in 69 BCE into the Ptolemaic dynasty, a Greek family that had ruled Egypt for nearly 300 years since the time of Alexander the Great. Surprisingly, she was the first Ptolemaic ruler who even bothered to learn the Egyptian language! Previous rulers had only spoken Greek and considered themselves superior to their Egyptian subjects.

Cleopatra became pharaoh at age 18, but she wasn't content to be just another puppet ruler while Rome took over the Mediterranean world. She was determined to restore Egypt's independence and greatness through a combination of diplomacy, intelligence, and strategic alliances.

Her alliances with Julius Caesar and later Mark Antony weren't just romantic relationships—they were brilliant political moves. Cleopatra understood that Egypt needed powerful Roman allies to survive, and she used her charm, intelligence, and political skills to forge partnerships that could have restored Egypt to its former glory.

But Cleopatra's dreams ended in disaster at the Battle of Actium in 31 BCE, where Octavian (later Emperor Augustus) defeated the combined forces of Cleopatra and Mark Antony. Rather than be captured and paraded through Rome as a prisoner, Cleopatra chose to end her life by allowing a poisonous asp to bite her.

With her death, Egypt became a Roman province, ending over 3,000 years of pharaonic rule. Cleopatra was truly the last pharaoh of Egypt, and she went down fighting to preserve her kingdom's independence.

Nefertiti: The Beautiful Queen Who May Have Ruled

Queen Nefertiti was the wife of the revolutionary pharaoh Akhenaten, and she may have been one of the most powerful women

in ancient Egypt. Her name means "the beautiful one has come," and her famous bust, discovered in 1912, shows an elegant woman with perfect features that has become an icon of ancient Egyptian art.

But Nefertiti was much more than just a beautiful face. She played a crucial role in Akhenaten's religious revolution, appearing prominently in temple art and ceremonies dedicated to the sun god Aten. Some scenes show her performing religious rituals that were usually reserved for pharaohs, suggesting she held unprecedented power for a queen.

Even more intriguingly, some scholars believe that after Akhenaten's death, Nefertiti may have ruled Egypt in her own right under a different name. This would make her one of the few women to achieve full pharaonic power, though the evidence is still debated by historians.

What's certain is that Nefertiti was a key figure in one of ancient Egypt's most dramatic periods, when the entire religious and artistic tradition of the kingdom was turned upside down.

Nefertari: The Beloved Queen

Nefertari was the principal wife of Ramses II, and she may have been the most beloved queen in Egyptian history. Ramses, who wasn't known for his modesty about anything, called her "the one for whom the sun shines" and built her one of the most beautiful tombs ever created.

Nefertari's tomb in the Valley of the Queens is considered one of the finest examples of ancient Egyptian art. The walls are covered with gorgeous paintings showing the queen's journey through the afterlife, and the colors are so well-preserved that they look like they were painted yesterday.

But Nefertari wasn't just a passive figure who looked pretty in art. She played an active role in diplomacy, corresponding directly with the queen of the Hittites to help negotiate the famous peace treaty between Egypt and the Hittite Empire. This makes her one of the first women in history whose diplomatic correspondence still survives.

Ramses also built a temple for Nefertari at Abu Simbel, right next to his own massive temple. The fact that he honored his wife with her own temple shows just how much he valued her partnership in ruling Egypt.

Tiye: The Power Behind the Throne

Queen Tiye was the wife of Pharaoh Amenhotep III and the mother of Akhenaten, and she may have been the most politically influential woman of her time. Foreign kings wrote directly to her, treating her as an equal partner in Egypt's government rather than just the pharaoh's wife.

Tiye came from a non-royal family, but her intelligence and political skills made her one of the most powerful people in Egypt. She continued to wield influence even after her husband's death, serving as an advisor to her revolutionary son Akhenaten.

Archaeological evidence suggests that Tiye lived to see the end of Akhenaten's religious experiment and may have played a role in the restoration of traditional Egyptian religion under Tutankhamun, who was probably her grandson.

🟨 Why Egypt's Women Had More Power

Egyptian women enjoyed rights that were rare in the ancient world:

- **Property rights**—Could own land, businesses, and slaves
- **Legal equality**—Could sue, make contracts, and testify in court
- **Divorce rights**—Could divorce husbands and keep their property
- **Religious roles**—Could serve as priestesses and temple officials
- **Royal succession**—Could inherit and pass on royal power

This made Egypt unique among ancient civilizations!

The women of ancient Egypt prove that female leadership wasn't just possible—it was often exceptional. From Hatshepsut's peaceful prosperity to Cleopatra's brilliant diplomacy, from Nefertiti's religious partnership to Nefertari's international correspondence, these women showed that power, intelligence, and political skill weren't limited by gender.

Their stories remind us that throughout history, when women have been given the opportunity to lead, they've often proven to be just as capable, creative, and effective as their male counterparts. The pharaohs we met in the previous chapter were remarkable rulers, but Egypt's powerful women were equally impressive in their own unique ways.

Next, we'll explore the incredible monuments that these pharaohs and queens built to ensure their eternal fame—the amazing pyramids that still amaze us today...

Chapter 5
Pyramids: Mountains for the Dead

Standing in the desert outside Cairo, Egypt, three massive stone structures rise from the sand like artificial mountains. The largest contains over 2 million stone blocks, each weighing as much as a car. It was the tallest building in the world for nearly 4,000 years—until the Eiffel Tower was built in 1889.

These are the pyramids of Giza, and they represent one of humanity's greatest achievements. But why did ancient Egyptians spend decades building these massive monuments? And how did they do it without modern machinery?

Houses for Eternity

To understand pyramids, you need to understand how ancient Egyptians thought about death. They didn't see death as an ending—they saw it as a journey to another life. But for this journey to be successful, the pharaoh's body needed to be preserved and protected forever.

Early Egyptian rulers were buried in simple rectangular tombs called mastabas. But as pharaohs became more powerful, they wanted grander monuments. Around 2630 BCE, a brilliant architect named Imhotep had a revolutionary idea: what if they stacked several mastabas on top of each other, making each level smaller than the one below?

The result was the Step Pyramid of Djoser—the world's first pyramid. It rose 200 feet into the air and amazed everyone who saw it. But this was just the beginning.

The Great Pyramid: Wonder of the Ancient World

The most famous pyramid is the Great Pyramid of Giza, built for Pharaoh Khufu around 2580 BCE. Originally standing 481 feet tall (about as high as a 48-story building), it was made from approximately 2.3 million stone blocks.

Here's what makes the Great Pyramid incredible: each stone block weighs between 2.5 and 15 tons. The largest granite stones weigh up to 80 tons—heavier than 50 cars! Yet these massive blocks fit together so precisely that you can't slide a knife blade between them.

The Great Pyramid was one of the Seven Wonders of the Ancient World, and it's the only one still standing today. For nearly 4,000 years, it held the record as the world's tallest human-made structure.

Inside the Pyramid

The interior of the Great Pyramid is just as impressive as the outside. A network of passages and chambers winds through the massive structure. The main burial chamber, called the King's Chamber, sits almost exactly in the center of the pyramid and contains a granite sarcophagus where Khufu's mummy was placed.

The pyramid also has a Grand Gallery—a soaring corridor with a ceiling 28 feet high. The precision here is incredible; the walls are perfectly straight and the ceiling stones fit together flawlessly.
Surprisingly, despite all the treasure that was surely buried with Khufu, the pyramid was empty when archaeologists explored it.

Grave robbers had broken in thousands of years ago and stolen everything valuable. This became a major problem—which is why later pharaohs started building hidden tombs in the Valley of the Kings instead of obvious pyramids.

Building the Impossible

So how did ancient Egyptians build something so massive without modern technology? For years, people thought it must have been impossible—some even claimed aliens helped! But archaeologists have uncovered the real secrets.

First, the Egyptians were master planners. Building a pyramid took about 20 years and required thousands of workers. The project needed architects, engineers, stone cutters, transporters, and countless laborers, all working together.

The stones came from quarries both nearby and hundreds of miles away. Local limestone was quarried close to the pyramid site, but fine white limestone for the outer casing came from across the Nile, and granite for internal chambers was transported from Aswan, over 500 miles south.

To move these massive stones, workers used copper tools, wooden levers, ropes, and lots of human muscle power. They built ramps—some straight, some zigzagging around the pyramid—to haul the blocks to higher levels. Recent discoveries suggest they used both external ramps and internal spiral ramps built right into the pyramid.

Pyramid Evolution: Learning by Trial and Error

Not all pyramids were as successful as the Great Pyramid. The ancient Egyptians learned by making mistakes, and some of those mistakes are still visible today.

The Bent Pyramid at Dahshur got its weird name because the builders changed the angle halfway up, making it look bent. They probably realized the original angle was too steep and the pyramid might collapse under its own weight.

The Red Pyramid, also at Dahshur, was the first successful "true" pyramid with smooth sides from bottom to top. This success led directly to the building of the Great Pyramid.

Over time, pyramid building became less common. They were incredibly expensive, took too long to build, and were obvious targets for tomb robbers. The last royal pyramids were built around 1650 BCE, though some pharaohs continued to build smaller pyramids later.

Workers, Not Slaves

One of the biggest myths about pyramid building is that slaves built them. This makes for dramatic movies, but it's not true. The pyramids were actually built by paid workers—mostly farmers who worked on construction projects during the Nile's flood season when they couldn't work their fields.

Archaeologists have found the workers' villages near the pyramids, complete with bakeries, breweries, and medical facilities. The workers ate well—beef, fish, bread, and beer were regular parts of their diet. Some workers were even buried near the pyramids they helped build, showing they were respected members of society.

The Mysterious Sphinx

Standing guard near the Great Pyramid is the Great Sphinx—a massive sculpture with the body of a lion and the head of a human (probably Pharaoh Khafre). This incredible statue is 240 feet long and 66 feet high, carved from a single piece of limestone.

The Sphinx is older than many pyramids and has been buried and uncovered by sand multiple times throughout history.

Pyramids Around the World

Egypt wasn't the only place where people built pyramids. The Maya in Central America, the Aztecs in Mexico, and various cultures in South America all built pyramid-like structures. But none matched the size, precision, or longevity of the Egyptian pyramids, which remain some of the most impressive monuments ever built.

How did they build something so huge
without modern machines?

The secret was organization and clever engineering:

- **Ramps:** Built ramps to move stones to higher levels
- **Levers and rollers:** Used wooden tools to move heavy blocks
- **Teamwork:** Groups of 20 men could move a 2.5-ton block using ropes
- **Precision planning:** Measured everything carefully using ropes and math
- **Seasonal workforce:** Farmers worked during flood season when they couldn't farm

No aliens needed—just smart people working together!

The pyramids represent more than just tombs for dead pharaohs—they're proof of what humans can accomplish when they combine vision, determination, and teamwork. These ancient monuments have survived wars, earthquakes, and thousands of years of weathering, continuing to inspire people to dream big and build something that lasts forever.

Next, we'll meet the gods and goddesses who the ancient Egyptians believed ruled over both the living and the dead...

CHAPTER 6
Gods and Goddesses

Imagine a world where gods have the heads of animals, where the sun is a golden boat sailing across the sky, and where a feather could determine whether you spend eternity in paradise or get eaten by a monster. Welcome to ancient Egyptian religion—one of the most colorful and fascinating belief systems ever created.

The ancient Egyptians didn't just believe in one god or even a few gods. They worshipped hundreds of deities, each with their own personality, powers, and stories. Some looked like humans, others had animal heads, and a few could change their shape at will. Together, these gods controlled everything from the weather and the Nile's floods to love, war, and what happened after death.

Ra: The King of the Gods

The most important god in ancient Egypt was Ra, the sun god. Every day, Ra sailed across the sky in his golden solar boat, bringing light and warmth to the world. When night came, he traveled through the underworld, battling the forces of darkness to ensure the sun would rise again.

Ra was usually depicted as a man with the head of a falcon, crowned with a solar disk. He was so important that many pharaohs included "Ra" in their names—like Ramses (meaning "Ra is the one who bore him") and Khafre (meaning "Ra appears").

According to Egyptian mythology, Ra created himself from the waters of chaos and then created other gods by speaking their names or through his tears. The ancient Egyptians believed that all life came from Ra, and without him, the world would return to darkness and chaos.

Osiris: Lord of the Afterlife

If Ra ruled the world of the living, Osiris ruled the realm of the

dead. Osiris was one of the most beloved gods because he offered hope that death wasn't the end—it was just the beginning of a new and better life.

The story of Osiris is one of the most famous myths in Egyptian religion. According to legend, Osiris was once a good and wise king of Egypt. His jealous brother Set murdered him, cut his body into pieces, and scattered them across Egypt. Osiris's wife, Isis, searched for the pieces and used her magical powers to bring him back to life. Although Osiris couldn't return to the world of the living, he became the ruler of the afterlife, where he judged the souls of the dead.

Osiris was usually shown as a mummified man with green or black skin (representing rebirth and fertile soil), holding the crook and flail that symbolized royal authority. Pharaohs believed they would become one with Osiris after death.

Isis: The Mother Goddess

Isis was one of the most powerful and beloved goddesses in ancient Egypt. She was the wife of Osiris, the mother of Horus, and the goddess of magic, motherhood, and healing. Her story of bringing Osiris back to life made her a symbol of loyalty, love, and the power of family bonds.

Egyptian women especially looked up to Isis as a protector and role model. She was often depicted as a woman with outstretched wings, symbolizing her protection over all of Egypt. Sometimes she was shown nursing her baby son Horus—an image that later influenced Christian art depicting Mary and Jesus.

Isis was also known as a master of magic and medicine. People believed she could heal the sick, protect travelers, and even bring the dead back to life. Her worship eventually spread far beyond Egypt to temples throughout the Roman Empire.

Anubis: Guide to the Afterlife

One of the most recognizable Egyptian gods is Anubis, the jackal-headed god of mummification and the afterlife. Anubis was responsible for protecting the dead and guiding them through the dangerous journey to the afterlife.

Why a jackal? Ancient Egyptians noticed that jackals often prowled around cemeteries, so they associated these animals with death and the afterlife. But Anubis wasn't scary—he was a protector who made sure the dead were properly prepared for their eternal journey.

Anubis played a crucial role in the famous "weighing of the heart" ceremony. When someone died, Anubis would weigh their heart against a feather of truth. If the heart was lighter than the feather (meaning the person had lived a good life), they could enter the afterlife. If the heart was heavier (weighed down by bad deeds), it would be devoured by Ammit, a monster with the head of a crocodile, the body of a lion, and the hindquarters of a hippopotamus.

Bastet: The Cat Goddess

Ancient Egyptians loved cats, and they had a goddess to prove it. Bastet, often depicted as a cat or a woman with a cat's head, was the goddess of cats, protection, and fertility. She was also associated with music, dancing, and joy.

Cats were so sacred to Bastet that killing one, even accidentally, was punishable by death. When family cats died, Egyptians would mummify them and mourn them just like human family members. Archaeologists have found thousands of mummified cats in ancient Egyptian tombs.

The city of Bubastis was the center of Bastet's worship, and every year thousands of people would travel there for a festival in her honor. According to historians, these festivals were among the biggest and most joyful celebrations in all of Egypt.

Temples: Houses of the Gods

The gods didn't live in heaven—they lived in temples. Each major city had a temple dedicated to its patron god, and these temples were considered the actual earthly homes of the deities.

Egyptian temples were massive, beautiful complexes with towering walls, elaborate carvings, and countless statues. Only priests and pharaohs were allowed into the innermost chambers where the god's statue resided. Three times a day, priests would "feed" the god by offering food, wash and dress the statue, and perform rituals to keep the god happy.

The most famous temple complex is at Karnak, dedicated to the god Amun-Ra. This enormous site covers over 200 acres and contains temples, chapels, and obelisks built over more than 1,000 years.

Daily Religious Life

Religion wasn't just something that happened in temples—it was part of everyday life for ancient Egyptians. People wore amulets with the symbols of their favorite gods, said prayers before meals, and made offerings at small household shrines.

Many Egyptians had personal relationships with specific gods. A mother might pray to Isis for protection during childbirth, a scribe would ask Thoth for wisdom, and a farmer might offer thanks to Hapi (the god of the Nile flood) for a good harvest.

Egyptian God Guide

- **Ra**—Falcon head, solar disk | **Powers:** Sun, creation, kingship
- **Osiris**—Mummified man, green/black skin | **Powers:** Afterlife, resurrection
  Isis—Woman with wings | **Powers:** Magic, motherhood, healing
- **Anubis**—Jackal head | **Powers:** Mummification, afterlife guide
- **Bastet**—Cat head | **Powers:** Cats, protection, joy

The gods and goddesses of ancient Egypt weren't distant, scary figures—they were like a huge, powerful family that cared about human affairs. They could be loving or angry, helpful or demanding, but they were always present in Egyptian life.

Understanding these gods helps us understand how ancient Egyptians saw their world: as a place where the divine and human realms were closely connected, where every aspect of life had meaning, and where death was not an ending but a transformation into something even better.

These beliefs about gods and the afterlife led to one of ancient Egypt's most famous practices—the preservation of the dead through mummification.

Next, we'll unwrap the mysteries of mummies and discover why ancient Egyptians spent so much time and effort preparing for death...

Chapter 7
Mummies and Tombs

Of all the things ancient Egypt is famous for, nothing captures our imagination quite like mummies. These perfectly preserved bodies, wrapped in linen bandages and placed in elaborate coffins, seem almost magical. But mummification wasn't about magic—it was about love, hope, and an unshakeable belief that death was just the beginning of an even better life.

Why Make Mummies?

To understand mummification, you need to think like an ancient Egyptian. They believed that every person had several different souls, including the "ka" (life force) and the "ba" (personality). After death, these souls needed to reunite with the body to live forever in the afterlife. But there was a problem: if the body decayed, the souls would have nowhere to go, and the person would truly die.

The solution was mummification—preserving the body so perfectly that it could last forever. This wasn't just for pharaohs and wealthy nobles. Anyone who could afford it wanted to be mummified, from scribes and merchants to craftsmen and farmers. Even beloved pets were mummified so they could join their owners in the afterlife.

The 70-Day Process

Creating a mummy was a complex process that took about 70 days and required the skills of highly trained specialists. The process was so sacred that it was performed by priests, not just regular workers.

Days 1-15: Preparing the Body First, the body was washed with wine and spices. Then came the most delicate part: removing the internal organs. Using a long, thin tool, embalmers removed the brain through the nose (they didn't think the brain was important, so they usually threw it away). Next, they made a small cut in the left side of the abdomen and carefully removed the liver, lungs, stomach, and intestines.

These organs were cleaned, dried, and placed in special containers called canopic jars. Each jar was protected by a different god: Imsety (human-headed) guarded the liver, Hapi (baboon-headed) protected the lungs, Duamutef (jackal-headed) watched over the stomach, and Qebehsenuef (falcon-headed) protected the intestines. The heart was left in the body because Egyptians believed it was needed for judgment in the afterlife.

Days 16-55: The Drying Process The empty body was then covered completely in natron, a type of salt found naturally in Egypt. This salt absorbed all the moisture from the body, preventing decay. The body was left buried in natron for about 40 days until it was completely dried out.

Days 56-70: Wrapping and Final Preparation After drying, the body was cleaned and stuffed with sawdust, linen, or other materials to give it a more lifelike shape. Then began the famous wrapping process. Using hundreds of yards of linen strips, embalmers carefully wrapped every finger, toe, and limb separately before wrapping the entire body.

Between the layers of wrapping, they placed amulets—magical charms designed to protect the deceased in the afterlife. The most important was the heart scarab, placed over the heart, which was inscribed with spells to ensure the heart wouldn't testify against the person during judgment.

Finally, a mask was placed over the head. For pharaohs, this might be made of gold (like Tutankhamun's famous mask), but ordinary people had masks made of cartonnage—a material similar to papier-mâché.

Tutankhamun's Incredible Tomb

The most famous mummy discovery happened in 1922 when British archaeologist Howard Carter found the tomb of Tutankhamun in the Valley of the Kings. When Carter first peered through a small hole into the tomb and was asked what he could see, he famously replied, "Wonderful things!"

Tut's tomb contained over 5,000 objects, including three nested coffins (the innermost made of solid gold), chariots, jewelry, furniture, clothing, food, and even board games for entertainment in the afterlife. The tomb had four rooms packed floor to ceiling with treasures.

The discovery made headlines around the world and sparked "Tut-mania"—a craze for all things Egyptian that influenced fashion, architecture, and popular culture throughout the 1920s. When scientists unwrapped Tutankhamun's mummy, they found 143 pieces of jewelry and amulets wrapped within the bandages, including his famous golden dagger.

Animal Mummies

Humans weren't the only ones who got mummified. Ancient Egyptians mummified millions of animals, from sacred cats and birds to crocodiles, bulls, and even fish. Some animals were

mummified because they were considered sacred to specific gods—like cats for Bastet or ibises for Thoth.

Pet animals were mummified so they could accompany their owners to the afterlife. Wealthy Egyptians might mummify their favorite cat, dog, or monkey and bury it in their tomb with its own miniature coffin.

But the animal mummy business also became a huge industry. Pilgrims visiting temples could buy mummified animals as offerings to the gods. Unfortunately, many of these were fakes—X-rays have revealed that some "animal mummies" contain nothing but sticks, stones, or random bones instead of complete animals.

Modern Mummy Science

Today, scientists study ancient mummies using high-tech tools that don't require unwrapping them. CT scans can show what's inside the wrappings, revealing details about how the person lived and died. We can learn about their health, diet, diseases, and injuries.

Some amazing discoveries have come from mummy research: evidence of ancient dental work, proof of diseases that still exist today, and even traces of foods people ate thousands of years ago. Scientists have found that ancient Egyptians suffered from many of the same health problems we do today, including heart disease, arthritis, and broken bones.

DNA analysis of mummies has also revealed family relationships among pharaohs and shown how different populations in ancient Egypt were related to modern Egyptians.

The Curse of the Mummy?

Ever since King Tut's tomb was opened, people have talked about "the curse of the mummy." Several people connected to the excavation died in the years following the discovery, leading to rumors that disturbing the pharaoh's rest had brought supernatural revenge.

But scientists point out that these deaths had natural explanations, and many people involved in the excavation lived long, healthy lives. Howard Carter himself, who actually opened the tomb, lived for 17 more years after the discovery. The "curse" was probably just coincidence, helped along by newspapers looking for exciting stories.

What would you take into the afterlife?
Ancient Egyptians packed their tombs with everything they thought they'd need:

- **Food and drink**—bread, beer, wine, honey, dried meat
- **Clothing and jewelry**—finest linens, gold ornaments, precious stones
- **Games and entertainment**—board games like senet, musical instruments
- **Tools and weapons**—for protection and daily activities
- **Personal items**—makeup, mirrors, combs, favorite possessions

What would you want to take? Remember, Egyptians believed the afterlife would be like the best version of life on Earth!

Mummification represents one of humanity's most elaborate attempts to defeat death. For over 3,000 years, ancient Egyptians perfected the art of preservation, driven by love for their families and faith in eternal life. The mummies they created have given us an incredible window into ancient Egyptian life, allowing us to meet these fascinating people face to face across thousands of years.

Next, we'll step away from the world of pharaohs and gods to discover what daily life was really like for ordinary people in ancient Egypt...

CHAPTER 8
Daily Life in Ancient Egypt

While pharaohs lived in golden palaces and priests performed sacred rituals in massive temples, most ancient Egyptians lived much simpler lives. They were farmers and fishermen, bakers and brewers, potters and weavers. They worried about their families, worked hard to make a living, and found joy in simple pleasures like good food, music, and time with friends.

Let's step into their world and discover what it was really like to be an ordinary person in ancient Egypt.

The Social Pyramid

Ancient Egyptian society was organized like a pyramid, with the pharaoh at the top and slaves at the bottom. But unlike a stone pyramid, people could sometimes move up or down this social ladder based on their talents, luck, or hard work.

At the very top was the pharaoh and the royal family. Just below them were high-ranking officials, priests, and nobles who owned large estates and lived in luxury.

The middle class included scribes, craftsmen, merchants, and lower-level priests. These people were respected because they had special skills that others needed. A talented scribe could work his way up to become a government official, and a skilled craftsman might become wealthy creating beautiful objects for the elite.

The largest group by far were farmers, laborers, and servants—

about 80% of the population. They worked the land, built the monuments, and performed the countless daily tasks that kept Egyptian civilization running.

At the bottom were slaves, though slavery was different in Egypt than in other cultures. Many "slaves" were prisoners of war who could eventually earn their freedom, and some were treated almost like family members.

Home Sweet Home

Most Egyptians lived in simple houses made of mud bricks. These bricks were made by mixing Nile mud with straw, pressing the mixture into wooden molds, and drying them in the sun. Mud brick was perfect for Egypt's climate—it kept houses cool during hot days and warm during chilly nights.

A typical Egyptian house had a flat roof that families used as extra living space. People would sleep on the roof during hot summer nights, dry food there, and even keep small animals like goats or chickens. Houses usually had just a few rooms: a main living area, one or two bedrooms, and a kitchen.

The wealthy lived in much larger houses with multiple stories, courtyards, gardens, and pools. These mansions might have dozens of rooms, including guest quarters, workshops, and shrines for worshipping household gods.

Fashion and Beauty

Ancient Egyptians loved to look good, and both men and women

spent considerable time on their appearance. The basic clothing was simple but elegant: men wore kilts (short skirts) made of linen, while women wore long, straight dresses, also made of linen.

Linen was perfect for Egypt's hot climate because it was light, breathable, and easy to wash. The quality of linen showed a person's status—wealthy people wore fine, almost transparent linen that was bleached pure white, while poor people wore coarser, darker fabric.

Both men and women wore jewelry whenever they could afford it. Gold was the most prized metal because it didn't tarnish and was believed to be the flesh of the gods. People wore rings, bracelets, necklaces, and earrings, often decorated with colorful stones like turquoise and lapis lazuli.

Makeup was essential for both men and women. They lined their eyes with black kohl and green malachite. This wasn't just for beauty—the makeup helped protect their eyes from the bright desert sun and may have helped prevent eye infections. They also painted their lips and cheeks with red ochre and used perfumes made from flowers and spices.

Family Life and Children

Family was extremely important in ancient Egypt. Most marriages were arranged by parents, but couples seem to have genuinely

cared for each other. Egyptian art often shows husbands and wives holding hands or embracing, and love poems from ancient Egypt reveal deep romantic feelings.

Egyptian children were treasured and loved. Parents wanted many children because children were expected to care for their parents in old age and ensure they were properly buried and remembered after death. Infant mortality was high, so having multiple children increased the chances that some would survive to adulthood.

Young children of both sexes wore their hair in a distinctive style called the "sidelock of youth"—their heads were shaved except for one long braid on the side. Children didn't wear clothes until they were about six years old (it was too hot, and cloth was expensive), and they often wore good-luck amulets to protect them from disease and accidents.

A Day in the Life of an Egyptian Child

Sunrise: Wake up on the roof where the family slept to escape the heat

Morning: Eat bread and weak beer for breakfast, help carry water from the Nile

School time: If you're lucky enough to go to scribe school, practice writing hieroglyphs on limestone

Midday: Rest during the hottest part of the day, maybe swim in the Nile

Afternoon: Help with family work—farming, weaving, or learning a trade

Evening: Family dinner, listen to stories about the gods, sleep under the stars

Children played with toys that would seem familiar today: dolls, balls, spinning tops, and board games. They also played physical games like wrestling, swimming, and tug-of-war. Wealthier children had more elaborate toys, including wooden animals with moving parts and miniature furniture for their dolls.

Education and Jobs

Most Egyptian children didn't go to school—they learned by helping their parents with work. Boys typically learned their father's trade, whether farming, carpentry, or metalworking. Girls learned household skills like cooking, weaving, and child care from their mothers.

However, some boys (and very rarely, girls) learned to read and write by attending scribe schools. Becoming a scribe was one of the best ways to move up in Egyptian society. Students learned by copying texts on pieces of limestone or broken pottery (papyrus was too expensive for practice). School was strict—students who made mistakes might be beaten with sticks!

The ancient Egyptians had many specialized jobs: bakers, brewers, jewelers, carpenters, stone masons, painters, musicians, dancers, barbers, and doctors. Some jobs required years of training and were highly respected.

Food and Drink

The ancient Egyptian diet was based on bread and beer—not just for adults, but for children too (the beer was very weak and safer to drink than water). Bread came in dozens of varieties, from simple flat loaves to fancy shapes for special occasions.

Egyptians also ate lots of vegetables: onions, garlic, leeks, lettuce, cucumbers, and beans. Fruits included dates, figs, grapes, and pomegranates. Those who lived near the Nile caught fish and hunted birds. Wealthier people ate beef, lamb, goat, and duck, while ordinary people rarely ate meat except during festivals.

Honey was the main sweetener (sugar didn't exist yet), and people flavored their food with herbs and spices. They cooked in clay pots over fires made from dried animal dung (wood was scarce in Egypt).

Entertainment and Fun

Despite their hard work, ancient Egyptians knew how to have fun. Music and dancing were popular at parties and festivals. Musicians played harps, flutes, drums, and rattles, while dancers performed elaborate routines.

Board games were incredibly popular. The most famous was senet, played on a board with 30 squares. The game had religious significance—winning represented successfully navigating the afterlife—but it was also just fun to play.

Religious festivals were the biggest celebrations of the year. During these festivals, work stopped, free food and beer were distributed, and everyone participated in processions, music, and dancing.

How was kid life different then vs. now?

Similar: Kids played games, had toys, loved their families, and got in trouble sometimes!

Different: No school for most kids, no clothes until age 6, married as teenagers, drank beer instead of juice, boys and girls had very different futures

---

Life in ancient Egypt wasn't easy, but it wasn't grim either. People found ways to enjoy themselves, care for their families, and take pride in their work. The rhythm of life followed the Nile's seasons in an endless cycle that connected every Egyptian to the river that made their civilization possible.

Whether you were a farmer's child playing in the mud or a nobleman's daughter learning to manage a household, you grew up knowing you were part of something amazing—a great civilization that had lasted for thousands of years.

Next, we'll explore one of ancient Egypt's greatest gifts to the world: the art of writing in pictures called hieroglyphs...

Chapter 9
Writing in Pictures: Hieroglyphs

Imagine trying to write your name using pictures of birds, eyes, water ripples, and baskets. Imagine reading a story where some symbols represent sounds, others represent whole words, and still others are just there to help you understand what you're reading about. Welcome to the fascinating world of hieroglyphs—ancient Egypt's system of writing in pictures.

For over 3,000 years, hieroglyphs covered the walls of temples, filled papyrus scrolls, and decorated everything from royal monuments to ordinary household items. Then, mysteriously, the knowledge of how to read them disappeared. For more than 1,400 years, these beautiful symbols remained silent—until one brilliant discovery changed everything.

The Birth of Writing

Around 3200 BCE, something revolutionary happened in ancient Egypt: people began using pictures to represent words and sounds. This made Egypt one of the first civilizations in the world to develop a complete writing system.

The word "hieroglyph" comes from Greek words meaning "sacred carving," because the Greeks saw these symbols carved on temple walls and assumed they were only used for religious purposes. But hieroglyphs were used for everything—government records, love letters, medical texts, stories, shopping lists, and even ancient Egyptian jokes!

The earliest hieroglyphs were simple pictures: a bird meant "bird," a house meant "house," and waves meant "water." But the system quickly became much more sophisticated.

How Hieroglyphs Actually Worked

Here's where hieroglyphs get really interesting: the same symbol could work in three completely different ways.

1. Pictograms (Picture = Thing) Some hieroglyphs were simple pictures of what they represented. A drawing of a sun meant "sun," a bird meant "bird," and a house meant "house."

2. Phonograms (Picture = Sound) Many hieroglyphs represented sounds rather than objects. For example, the picture of a house (which sounded like "per" in ancient Egyptian) could be used whenever you needed the sound "per" in a word, even if the word had nothing to do with houses. It's like using a picture of a bee and a leaf to write "belief"—the pictures don't matter, just the sounds.

3. Determinatives (Picture = Category) Some hieroglyphs were silent helpers that told you what category you were reading about. A pair of walking legs meant the word had something to do with movement. A small man or woman symbol told you whether you were reading about a male or female person. These weren't pronounced—they just helped prevent confusion.

Reading Like an Ancient Egyptian

Ancient Egyptian scribes didn't make reading easy! Here were some challenges:

No Spaces Between Words: Imagine reading: "ANCIENTEGYPTIANSHADDIFFERENTRULESFORWRITING." That's what hieroglyphic texts looked like.

No Vowels: Egyptian writing mostly left out vowel sounds. You had to figure out from context whether "pr" meant "house," "to go out," or something else.

Multiple Directions: Hieroglyphs could be written left to right, right to left, or top to bottom. To figure out which direction to read, you looked at which way the animal and human figures were facing— they always looked toward the beginning of the line.

The Tools of Writing

Egyptian scribes used special tools for writing. For everyday writing, they used reed pens made from marsh plants. The reed was cut at an angle and chewed at the tip to make it soft and flexible. Ink was made from soot mixed with wa-

ter for black writing, and from red ochre for red writing. Scribes often used red ink for emphasis or to mark new sections.

For permanent inscriptions on stone, scribes first painted the hieroglyphs, then stone carvers used copper tools to cut each symbol into the rock. The carved symbols were often painted in bright colors.

Papyrus: Ancient Egypt's Paper

The Egyptians invented one of the world's first types of paper using the papyrus plant that grew in the Nile marshes. Making papyrus required skill and patience.

Workers cut papyrus stalks and peeled away the outer bark to reveal the core inside. They sliced this core into thin strips and laid them out in two layers—one horizontal and one vertical. The strips were then pressed together and dried in the sun, creating a writing surface that was strong and smooth.

Papyrus was expensive, so scribes often reused it by washing off old ink and writing new text on top. The word "paper" actually comes from "papyrus."

The Mystery Years

Around 400 CE, something dramatic happened: people stopped using hieroglyphs. The last known hieroglyphic inscription was carved in 394 CE. After that, the knowledge gradually disappeared.

Several factors contributed to this loss. Christianity spread through Egypt, and the new religion discouraged "pagan" Egyptian writing. The Roman government preferred Latin and Greek. A simpler form of Egyptian writing using Greek letters became more popular.

By 600 CE, no one alive could read the mysterious pictures that covered Egypt's monuments. For over 1,400 years, hieroglyphs remained one of history's greatest puzzles.

The Rosetta Stone: Key to the Past

In 1799, a French soldier named Pierre-François Bouchard made one of the most important archaeological discoveries in history. While working near the town of Rosetta, he found a large black stone covered with three different types of writing.

The Rosetta Stone contained the same text written in hieroglyphs at the top, Demotic (simplified Egyptian) in the middle, and ancient Greek at the bottom. This was exactly what scholars needed to crack the hieroglyphic code!

The text wasn't very exciting—it was a decree from 196 BCE praising King Ptolemy V. But having the same message in three scripts meant scholars could use the known Greek text to figure out what the hieroglyphs meant.

Jean-François Champollion: The Code Breaker

Many brilliant scholars worked on the Rosetta Stone, but the breakthrough came from a young French linguist named Jean-François Champollion. In 1822, after years of work, Champollion made the crucial discovery.

Previous scholars had assumed that hieroglyphs were purely symbolic—that each picture represented a whole idea. But Champollion realized that many hieroglyphs represented sounds, just like letters in our alphabet. By comparing the Greek and hieroglyphic versions of royal names like Ptolemy and Cleopatra, he figured out which hieroglyphs represented which sounds.

Champollion's breakthrough opened the floodgates. Once scholars understood that hieroglyphs could represent sounds as well as ideas, they quickly deciphered thousands of texts. Suddenly, ancient Egyptians could speak to us across the centuries.

What the Hieroglyphs Revealed

As scholars learned to read hieroglyphs, they discovered that ancient Egyptians had written about everything: medical texts, mathematical formulas, literature, historical records, and personal letters. We found love poems, adventure stories, and even complaints about lazy workers!

Try writing your name using these hieroglyphic sounds:

- A = (vulture)
- B = (foot)
- M = (owl)
- K = (basket)
- L = (lion)
- S = (cloth)
- T = (loaf)
- R = (mouth)
- N = (water)

Bonus: The hieroglyph message means "Good morning!" in ancient Egyptian.

The decipherment of hieroglyphs was like opening a time capsule sealed for over a thousand years. Ancient Egyptians weren't just mysterious pyramid builders—they were real people who could tell us their stories in their own words.

Today, scholars continue discovering and translating new hieroglyphic texts. Every temple wall and papyrus scroll has the potential to reveal new secrets about this fascinating civilization.

Next, we'll meet some of the most famous individuals from ancient Egypt, including remarkable people who achieved greatness through their talents rather than their royal birth...

Chapter 10
Beyond the Pharaohs: Other Amazing Egyptians

While pharaohs ruled from golden thrones and built massive pyramids, some of ancient Egypt's most fascinating people were ordinary citizens who achieved extraordinary things. These weren't born into royal families or handed power by their parents. They earned their place in history through talent, courage, wisdom, and determination.

Let's meet some remarkable Egyptians who prove that greatness can come from anywhere—and that sometimes the most interesting stories belong to people whose names almost nobody knows today.

Imhotep: The Genius Who Became a God

Nearly 4,500 years ago, a man named Imhotep achieved something almost impossible: he became famous not for being born into royalty, but for his incredible talents. Imhotep served Pharaoh Djoser around 2650 BCE, but he wasn't a prince or nobleman—he was a commoner who rose to greatness through pure ability.

Imhotep is credited with designing the Step Pyramid at Saqqara—the world's first pyramid. Before Imhotep, royal tombs were simple rectangular structures. His revolutionary idea to stack them on top of each other, getting smaller at each level, created something the world had never seen before. The Step Pyramid rose 200 feet into the air and amazed everyone who saw it.

But Imhotep was much
more than an architect. Ancient texts describe him as
a physician whose medical
knowledge was so advanced
that people traveled from
across the known world
to seek his treatment. He
was also a priest, poet, and
philosopher whose wisdom
sayings were quoted for centuries after his death.

Imhotep's reputation grew so great that 2,000 years after his
death, people were still worshipping him as a god of medicine
and wisdom. The Greeks identified him with their god of healing,
Asclepius. People left offerings at his shrine and prayed to him
for healing, making Imhotep one of the few non-royal Egyptians
ever to achieve divine status.

What made Imhotep extraordinary was that he proved talent
could triumph over birth. In a society where your family determined your future, Imhotep showed that brilliant minds could
rise to the very top.

Sinuhe: The Ancient World's Greatest Traveler

Imagine being so famous for your adventures that people are still
reading your story 4,000 years later. That's exactly what happened
to Sinuhe, whose tale became one of ancient Egypt's most popular pieces of literature.

Sinuhe was a court official who served under Pharaoh Amenem-
hat I around 1950 BCE. When the pharaoh died suddenly, Sinuhe

panicked and fled Egypt, fearing he might be caught up in political turmoil. What followed was an incredible journey that took him across the ancient Middle East.

Sinuhe's story, written in his own words, tells of his adventures in foreign lands. He fought duels with local champions, became a wealthy chieftain, married, and had children. But throughout his travels, he never stopped missing Egypt. After decades abroad, he sent a letter to the new pharaoh begging to return home.

The pharaoh welcomed Sinuhe back, and he spent his final years in Egypt, writing down his adventures. "The Story of Sinuhe" became so popular that copies have been found in schools throughout Egypt—it was apparently required reading for young scribes learning to read and write.

Sinuhe's story is remarkable because it's one of the first autobiographies ever written. It shows us that ancient Egyptians were curious about the wider world and that even 4,000 years ago, people dreamed of adventure and travel.

Amenemheb: The Soldier Who Saved a Pharaoh

Not all Egyptian heroes were architects or writers—some were warriors whose courage in battle earned them eternal fame. Amenemheb was a soldier who served under Pharaoh Thutmose III, one of Egypt's greatest military leaders, around 1450 BCE.

During one of Thutmose's campaigns in Syria, disaster struck. The pharaoh was hunting elephants when a massive bull elephant charged directly at him. The pharaoh was in mortal danger—one swipe from the elephant's trunk could have killed the most powerful man in Egypt.

That's when Amenemheb acted. The brave soldier threw himself between the pharaoh and the charging elephant, cutting off the beast's trunk with his sword and saving Thutmose's life. This single moment of incredible courage earned Amenemheb a place in Egyptian history.

But Amenemheb's heroics didn't stop there. During the siege of the city of Kadesh, he snuck into the enemy camp at night and stole the horses of the enemy prince, crippling their cavalry. His tomb inscription proudly lists his achievements: "I fought bravely in his majesty's presence in the southern and northern countries... I brought away living prisoners."

Amenemheb's story shows that ordinary soldiers could achieve greatness through bravery and loyalty. His tomb paintings depict him receiving gold necklaces and other rewards from a grateful pharaoh—proof that heroism was recognized and celebrated in ancient Egypt.

Rekhmire: The Power Behind the Throne

While pharaohs got all the glory, much of the real work of running Egypt was done by viziers—chief ministers who handled the day-to-day business of governing a complex civilization. The most famous vizier was Rekhmire, who served under Pharaohs Thutmose III and Amenhotep II around 1400 BCE.

Rekhmire's tomb is one of the most detailed sources we have about how ancient Egyptian government actually worked. The walls are covered with paintings showing him overseeing tax collection, judging legal cases, supervising construction projects, and managing Egypt's relations with foreign countries.

One painting shows Rekhmire receiving tribute from Nubia, Syria, and other lands—exotic animals, gold, precious stones, and beautiful crafts. Another shows him inspecting workshops where craftsmen make furniture, jewelry, and weapons for the pharaoh. Still others depict him managing the harvest and ensuring Egypt's food supply.

Rekhmire's tomb inscription includes his "job description": "I was the heart of the Lord, the ears and eyes of my sovereign. I was his efficient agent... Nothing occurred without my knowledge." Essentially, Rekhmire was running Egypt while the pharaoh focused on religious duties and military campaigns.

What makes Rekhmire fascinating is that his tomb gives us a behind-the-scenes look at how Egypt actually functioned. While pharaohs built pyramids and fought wars, it was people like Rekhmire who kept the civilization running day to day.

Khaemwaset: Egypt's First Archaeologist

Prince Khaemwaset was one of Ramses II's many sons, but instead of seeking power or military glory, he became fascinated with Egypt's ancient past. Living around 1250 BCE, Khaemwaset spent his life studying and restoring monuments that were already over 1,000 years old.

Khaemwaset traveled throughout Egypt, examining old pyramids, temples, and tombs. When he found structures that were crumbling or had been damaged, he organized restoration projects. He even left inscriptions explaining what he had done—making him history's first archaeologist!

One of his inscriptions reads: "It was the High Priest Khaemwaset who renewed the monument of King Unas, since he found it in ruins." Khaemwaset was essentially doing 3,000 years ago what museum curators do today—preserving the past for future generations.

What's remarkable about Khaemwaset is that he understood something many people in his time didn't: that Egypt's history was worth preserving. While others saw old monuments as sources of building stone, Khaemwaset saw them as treasures that told the story of his civilization.

Ordinary People, Extraordinary Lives

These amazing Egyptians prove that greatness isn't about being born into the right family:

- **Imhotep** rose from commoner to god through genius
- **Sinuhe** became famous through his writing and adventures
- **Amenemheb** earned eternal fame through a moment of incredible courage
- **Rekhmire** wielded enormous power through skill and intelligence
- **Khaemwaset** chose to preserve the past rather than seek personal glory

These remarkable Egyptians show us that ancient Egypt was full of talented, ambitious, and creative people at every level of society. While pharaohs ruled from their palaces, ordinary Egyptians were building, fighting, exploring, governing, and creating in ways that still inspire us today.

Their stories remind us that throughout history, the most interesting people are often those who achieve greatness not because of who they were born to be, but because of who they chose to become.

Next, we'll explore some of the strangest, most surprising, and downright bizarre aspects of ancient Egyptian life...

Chapter 11
Strange but True:
Egypt's Wildest Secrets

After learning about pharaohs and pyramids, gods and goddesses, you might think you know everything about ancient Egypt. But this remarkable civilization was full of surprises, bizarre customs, and downright weird practices that would seem absolutely crazy to us today. Get ready to discover the strangest, most amusing, and most unbelievable aspects of ancient Egyptian life—all of which are completely true!

The Crocodile God's Sacred Pets

The ancient Egyptians worshipped a crocodile god named Sobek, and at his temple in Crocodilopolis, they kept live crocodiles as sacred animals. But these weren't just any crocodiles—they were pampered like Egyptian royalty!

The sacred crocodiles wore golden earrings and bracelets, had their claws painted with nail polish, and were fed the finest foods including honey cakes, roasted meat, and wine. Priests would massage them with precious oils and perfumes. When these holy crocodiles died, they were mummified with the same care given to pharaohs and buried in elaborate tombs.

Visitors from around the ancient world came to see these blinged-out crocodiles. The Greek historian Herodotus wrote about watching priests feed wine to a sacred crocodile by prying open its jaws and pouring the wine directly down its throat. Imagine having that job!

Animal Mummy Madness

We've learned about human mummies, but the ancient Egyptians took animal mummification to absolutely wild extremes. Archaeologists have found mummified cats, dogs, birds, fish, crocodiles, bulls, sheep, baboons, and even beetles. But the scale was mind-boggling.

At one site called Tuna el-Gebel, archaeologists discovered galleries containing over 4 million mummified ibises (sacred birds of the god Thoth). The ancient Egyptians mummified so many cats that in the 1800s, a British company imported 180,000 cat mummies from Egypt to grind up as fertilizer for English farms!

Some wealthy Egyptians even mummified their pet goldfish. But here's the weird part: many animal mummies turned out to be fakes. When scientists X-rayed some "cat mummies," they found nothing but sticks, stones, or random animal bones wrapped up to fool paying customers.

Beauty Secrets That Would Shock You

Ancient Egyptians were obsessed with looking good, but some of their beauty treatments were absolutely bizarre by today's standards.

Both men and women wore elaborate eye makeup, but they didn't stop there. They used crocodile dung as face cream, believing it would give them smooth, youthful skin. They made lip gloss from crushed beetles mixed with animal fat. For deodorant, they rubbed their armpits with perfumed pellets made from ground-up ostrich eggs.

One beauty treatment involved putting fresh mouse brains on bald spots to cure baldness. Another "cure" for going bald was to rub your head with a mixture of lion fat, hippopotamus fat, crocodile fat, cat fat, snake fat, and ibex fat. Apparently, if you couldn't grow hair, you should at least smell like a zoo!

Egyptian dentists filled cavities with a mixture of honey, ground pearls, and crushed eggshells. While honey actually has antibacterial properties, imagine how painful it must have been to bite down on ground-up pearls.

The World's First Board Game Addicts

The ancient Egyptians loved board games so much that they buried game sets with their dead so they could keep playing in the afterlife. The most popular game was senet, played on a board with 30 squares arranged in three rows of ten.

Senet wasn't just entertainment—it had deep religious significance. The game represented the journey of the soul through the afterlife, and winning meant you had successfully navigated the dangers of death to reach eternal paradise. No pressure!

But Egyptians also played games just for fun. They had a game called "Hounds and Jackals" (like an ancient version of Chutes and Ladders), various dice games, and even an early form of bowling. Some Egyptian children played with yo-yos made from clay disks.

Archaeological evidence suggests that some Egyptians were serious gaming addicts. Several tombs contain multiple game sets, and some people were buried with ivory game pieces and gold-inlaid boards worth small fortunes.

Medical Practices: Brilliant and Bizarre

Ancient Egyptian medicine was surprisingly advanced in some ways and absolutely crazy in others. Egyptian doctors could perform surgery, set broken bones, and even do basic dentistry. They knew that the heart pumped blood and understood that the brain controlled thinking.

But their medical treatments often sound like something from a horror movie. For headaches, they recommended tying a clay crocodile holding grain in its mouth to the patient's head with a strip of linen. For constipation, the cure was an enema made from honey, sweet beer, and various unmentionable ingredients. One medical papyrus recommends treating a crying baby by giving it a mixture that included fly dirt and beer. For eye problems, they suggested a treatment involving pig's eyes, antimony, red ochre, and honey applied directly to the eyeball.

Perhaps strangest of all, they believed that the heart was the center of intelligence and emotion, while the brain was just useless stuffing. That's why during mummification, they carefully preserved the heart but threw the brain away!

The Great Pyramid's Mind-Blowing Facts

We've learned about pyramid construction, but some facts about the Great Pyramid are so incredible they seem impossible:
The Great Pyramid was originally covered in smooth, white limestone casing stones that made it shine like a mirror in the desert sun. The pyramid's base is so perfectly level that it varies by only 2.1 centimeters across its entire 756-foot width. The sides are aligned to true north with an accuracy that modern construction struggles to achieve!

If you took all the stone from the Great Pyramid and cut it into 12-inch cubes, you could build a wall 3 feet high that would stretch from New York to Los Angeles.

Weird Food Facts

The ancient Egyptian diet included some foods that would seem very strange to us today. They ate roasted locusts as snacks (apparently they taste like shrimp), regularly consumed various types of birds including flamingos and pelicans, and considered hedgehog meat a delicacy.

Egyptians were probably the first people to keep bees for honey production. Beer was so important that they had a goddess of beer named Tenenet. Workers building the pyramids received beer rations as part of their wages—about a gallon per person per day!

The Mystery of Egyptian Blue

The ancient Egyptians invented the world's first synthetic pigment: a brilliant blue color used in paintings and decorations. This "Egyptian blue" was made by heating sand, copper, and other materials to extremely high temperatures—a process so complex that the secret was lost after the fall of the Roman Empire.

Scientists have recently discovered that Egyptian blue has amazing properties: it glows under infrared light and can even conduct electricity! This ancient pigment is now being studied for use in modern solar panels. The ancient Egyptians accidentally invented a material that's still useful in the 21st century!

The Calendar Confusion

The ancient Egyptians created one of the world's first 365-day calendars, but they made one small mistake. Their year was exactly 365 days, but the actual solar year is 365.25 days. This meant their calendar slowly drifted out of sync with the seasons.

Over time, their "summer" festivals started happening in winter, and their flood predictions became completely wrong. The Egyptians knew about this problem but decided it wasn't worth fixing because they believed changing the calendar would anger the gods. It took them over 1,000 years to finally add an extra day every four years!

Quick Fire Amazing Egypt Facts

- Cleopatra lived closer to the Moon landing (1969) than to the Great Pyramid's construction!
- Ancient Egyptians invented toothpaste, breath mints, and bowling
- They had over 2,000 different gods and goddesses
- Some pharaohs were buried with 365 linen loincloths—one for each day of the year
- They used moldy bread as an antibiotic (which actually worked!)
- Egyptian women had more legal rights than women in most other ancient civilizations

What's amazing about these weird and wonderful facts is how they show that ancient Egyptians weren't so different from us. They loved their pets (maybe too much), were obsessed with looking good, got addicted to games, and came up with crazy solutions to everyday problems.

They were inventors who created things we still use today, but they were also people who believed that mouse brains could cure baldness and that crocodile dung made excellent face cream. They built monuments that have lasted for thousands of years, but they also spent fortunes mummifying their goldfish.

Perhaps that's what makes ancient Egypt so endlessly fascinating—it reminds us that human beings have always been a mixture of wisdom and silliness, genius and weirdness.

Finally, let's test how much you've learned about this incredible civilization...

Chapter 12
Test Your Egypt Knowledge

Congratulations! You've journeyed through 3,000 years of ancient Egyptian history, from the first pharaohs to the last. You've explored pyramids and tombs, met gods and goddesses, learned about daily life along the Nile, discovered amazing women rulers, and uncovered some of the weirdest facts about this incredible civilization.

Now it's time to test your knowledge and see how much you've learned about ancient Egypt. Don't worry—this isn't a scary school test! These activities are designed to be fun while helping you remember the amazing things you've discovered.

Would You Survive in Ancient Egypt?

Let's start with some scenarios that will test your understanding of ancient Egyptian life. For each situation, choose the best answer based on what you've learned.

Scenario 1: You're a young Egyptian and it's flooding season (Akhet). What should you do?
  A) Panic and run to higher ground—the flood will destroy everything!
  B) Celebrate! This is the best time of year when the Nile brings fertile soil
  C) Start planting crops immediately while the ground is wet
  D) Begin building a pyramid since you can't farm

Scenario 2: You want to become a scribe. What's the most important skill you need?
   A) How to speak Greek and Latin
   B) Advanced mathematics and engineering
   C) How to read and write hieroglyphs
   D) How to mummify bodies

Scenario 3: You're invited to dinner at a wealthy Egyptian's house. What should you expect?
   A) Pizza, hamburgers, and soda
   B) Bread, beer, vegetables, fish, and maybe some meat
   C) Only bread and water—Egyptians ate very little
   D) Exotic foods from around the world

Scenario 4: You want to become pharaoh but you're a woman. What's your best strategy?
   A) Give up—women could never rule Egypt
   B) Follow Hatshepsut's example and prove your leadership abilities
   C) Only marry a pharaoh and hope for the best
   D) Wait for modern times when women have more rights

Scenario 5: You die and want to be mummified. How long will the process take?
   A) One day—it's just wrapping the body
   B) One week of careful preparation
   C) About 70 days from start to finish
   D) One year to do it properly

True or False Challenge

Answer each question true or false.

1. The Great Pyramid was the tallest building in the world for almost 4,000 years.

2. Cleopatra was actually Greek, not Egyptian.

3. The pyramids were built by slaves.

4. Ancient Egyptians invented the world's first form of paper.

5. Egyptian children went to school just like kids today.

6. Ancient Egyptians mummified their pets.

7. Hieroglyphs are just pretty pictures with no real meaning.

8. Women could never rule as pharaohs in ancient Egypt.

9. Ancient Egyptians believed the heart was more important than the brain.

10. The Nile River flows from north to south.

Multiple Choice: Egyptian Experts

Choose the correct answer from the choices given.

1. What does the word "pharaoh" actually mean?
   A) Divine ruler B) Great house C) Son of Ra D) King of kings

2. Which god had the head of a jackal?
   A) Ra B) Horus C) Anubis D) Thoth

3. Who built the first pyramid?
   A) Khufu B) Imhotep C) Ramses II D) Tutankhamun

4. What was used to preserve mummies?
   A) Ice B) Special chemicals C) Natron salt D) Honey

5. Which female pharaoh wore a false beard?
  A) Cleopatra B) Nefertiti C) Hatshepsut D) Nefertari

Timeline Challenge

Put these events in chronological order (earliest to latest):

- Cleopatra's death (last pharaoh)
- Building of the Great Pyramid
- Step Pyramid built
- Discovery of Tutankhamun's tomb
- Hatshepsut's reign

Creative Thinking Questions

1. If you could meet any ancient Egyptian from this book, who would you choose and what would you ask them?

2. What do you think was ancient Egypt's greatest achievement? Why?

3. How would your life be different if you lived in ancient Egypt?

4. What lesson from ancient Egypt do you think is most important for people today?

Egyptian Word Bank

Match these Egyptian terms with their definitions:

Terms: Pharaoh, Hieroglyphs, Sarcophagus, Papyrus, Natron, Sphinx, Pyramid, Mummy

Definitions:
1. Ancient Egyptian writing using pictures
2. Stone container for a mummy
3. Salt used to preserve bodies
4. Ancient Egyptian paper made from reeds
5. Preserved dead body
6. Monument with a lion's body and human head
7. Ancient Egyptian ruler
8. Triangular tomb structure

Final Reflection: What Would You Remember Most?

Think about everything you've learned about ancient Egypt. If you had to tell a friend just three things about this incredible civilization, what would they be?

Your Three Most Important Facts:

Congratulations, Egyptian Explorer!

You've completed your journey through ancient Egypt! You've learned about the mighty Nile River, powerful pharaohs and queens, incredible pyramids, fascinating gods and goddesses, the amazing mummification process, daily life along the river, hieroglyphic writing, famous Egyptians who changed history, and strange but true facts that show how human these ancient people were.

More importantly, you've discovered that history isn't just about memorizing dates and names—it's about understanding how real people lived, what they believed, and what they achieved. The ancient Egyptians created one of humanity's greatest civilizations, and their legacy continues to influence our world today.

Whether you're interested in building pyramid models, learning to write your name in hieroglyphs, visiting an Egyptian museum, or just impressing your friends with amazing facts about crocodile gods and golden mummies, you now have the knowledge to appreciate one of history's most fascinating civilizations.

What Will You Explore Next?

Now that you've mastered ancient Egypt, you might be ready to explore other amazing civilizations:

- **Ancient Rome**—Gladiators, emperors, and the world's greatest empire
- **Ancient China**—The Great Wall, amazing inventions, and powerful dynasties
- **Medieval Times**—Knights, castles, and life in the Middle Ages

History is full of incredible stories waiting to be discovered!

ANSWERS

Would You Survive in Ancient Egypt?

Scenario 1
Answer: B—The annual flood was cause for celebration, not panic. It brought the rich soil that made farming possible.

Scenario 2
Answer: C—Scribes were valuable because they could read and write hieroglyphs. This skill opened doors to government jobs and social advancement.

Scenario 3
Answer: B—The Egyptian diet was based on bread and beer, supplemented with vegetables, fish, and occasionally meat for those who could afford it.

Scenario 4
Answer: B—Hatshepsut and other women proved that female pharaohs could be incredibly successful rulers.

Scenario 5
Answer: C—Mummification was a complex 70-day process involving removing organs, drying the body in natron, and careful wrapping.

True or False Challenge

1. *True*—It held the record from about 2580 BCE until the Eiffel Tower was built in 1889.

2. *True*—She belonged to the Ptolemaic dynasty and was the first ruler in her family to even learn Egyptian.

3. *False*—They were built by paid workers, mostly farmers who worked during flood season.

4. *True*—Papyrus was one of humanity's first writing materials.

5. *False*—Most children learned by working with their parents. Only a few went to scribe schools.

6. *True*—They mummified cats, dogs, birds, and even goldfish for the afterlife.

7. *False*—Hieroglyphs were a complex writing system representing sounds, words, and ideas.

8. *False*—Hatshepsut, Cleopatra, and possibly Nefertiti ruled as pharaohs.

9. *True*—They thought the heart controlled intelligence and emotion, while the brain was useless.

10. *False*—The Nile flows from south to north, toward the Mediterranean Sea.

Multiple Choice: Egyptian Experts
1. Answer: B—"Pharaoh" means "great house," referring to the palace.

2. Answer: C—Anubis, the god of mummification and guide to the afterlife.

3. Answer: B—Imhotep designed the Step Pyramid for Pharaoh Djoser.

4. Answer: C—Bodies were dried using natron, a naturally occurring salt.

5. Answer: C—Hatshepsut adopted male royal symbols including the false beard.

Timeline Challenge
Correct Order:
1. **Step Pyramid built** (c. 2630 BCE)
2. **Building of the Great Pyramid** (c. 2580 BCE)
3. **Hatshepsut's reign** (c. 1479-1458 BCE)
4. **Cleopatra's death** (30 BCE)
5. **Discovery of Tutankhamun's tomb** (1922 CE)

Creative Thinking Questions

1. *Sample thoughts: Meet Imhotep to learn about his architectural secrets, ask Hatshepsut about ruling as a woman, or talk to a pyramid worker about the construction process.*

2. *Sample thoughts: The pyramids show incredible engineering, hieroglyphs preserved knowledge for thousands of years, or their 3,000-year civilization showed remarkable stability.*

3. *Sample thoughts: No school for most kids, closer connection to family, but also harder physical work and less medical knowledge.*

4. *Sample thoughts: Working together to achieve great things, preserving knowledge for future generations, or respecting the environment.*

Egyptian Word Bank

Answers: 1-Hieroglyphs, 2-Sarcophagus, 3-Natron, 4-Papyrus, 5-Mummy, 6-Sphinx, 7-Pharaoh, 8-Pyramid

Final Score Check:

Egyptian Expert (90-100%): You're ready to lead your own archaeological expedition!

Pyramid Builder (75-89%): You've got solid knowledge of ancient Egypt

Apprentice Scribe (60-74%): Good work—you're learning the basics well

Desert Wanderer (Below 60%): Time to reread some chapters and try again!

Remember: The goal isn't to get every answer right, but to spark your curiosity about the incredible people and civilizations that came before us. Keep exploring, keep learning, and keep asking questions about our amazing world!

Want to Learn More About Ancient Egypt?

Websites

- **National Geographic Kids Egypt** (www.kids.nationalgeographic.com/history/ancient-egypt): Fun facts, games, and incredible photos of pyramids and mummies
- **BBC History for Kids: Ancient Egypt** (www.bbc.co.uk/history/ancient/egyptians/):Interactive timelines and cool activities about Egyptian life
- **Smithsonian's History Explorer** (historyexplorer.si.edu/egypt): Virtual museum tours and artifacts you can examine up close
- **World History for Kids: Ancient Egypt** (www.ducksters.com/history/ancient_egypt.php): Easy-to-understand articles and activities about Egyptian civilization

Books

- Boyer, Crispin. *Everything Ancient Egypt: Dig Into a Treasure Trove of Facts, Photos, and Fun.* National Geographic Children's Books, 2012.
- Hart, George. *Ancient Egypt* (DK Eyewitness). DK Children, 2014.
- Snyder, Zilpha Keatley. *The Egypt Game.* Yearling, 1997.
- Giblin, James Cross. *Secrets of the Sphinx.* Scholastic Press, 2004.

Museums to Visit

- **Metropolitan Museum of Art (New York City)**—Amazing Egyptian wing with real mummies
- **Field Museum (Chicago)**—Incredible pyramid and mummy exhibits
- **Museum of Fine Arts (Boston)**—Beautiful collection of Egyptian art and artifacts

- **Penn Museum (Philadelphia)**—Extensive Egyptian and Mesopotamian collections

Documentaries
- ***Egypt's Great Pyramid*** (National Geographic, 2017)
- **King Tut's Tomb** (Discovery Channel, 2019)

Activities
- Try writing your name in hieroglyphs using online translators
- Visit a local museum's Egyptian collection
- Build your own pyramid model
- Make papyrus paper using reeds or paper strips

GLOSSARY

Afterlife: The place ancient Egyptians believed people went after they died

Canopic Jars: Special containers used to hold the organs removed during mummification

Hieroglyph: Ancient Egyptian writing that used pictures and symbols to represent words and sounds

Mummy: A dead body that has been preserved using special salts and wrapping

Natron: A natural salt used by ancient Egyptians to dry out bodies during mummification

Nile River: The longest river in the world, which flows through Egypt and made their civilization possible

Papyrus: A reed plant that ancient Egyptians used to make the world's first paper

Pharaoh: The title for ancient Egyptian kings and queens, who were considered gods on Earth

Pyramid: A large stone monument with four triangular sides, built as tombs for pharaohs

Sarcophagus: A stone coffin, often decorated with carvings and paintings

Scribe: A person who could read and write hieroglyphs, making them very important in ancient Egypt

Shaduf: A simple machine with a pole, bucket, and weight used to lift water from the Nile

Sphinx: A creature with a human head and a lion's body, like the famous Great Sphinx near the pyramids

Temple: A building where ancient Egyptians worshipped their gods

Tomb: A special burial place where mummies and their treasures were placed

Vizier: The pharaoh's most important advisor, like a prime minister

A Note on Sources

The information presented in this book draws from widely accepted historical and archaeological scholarship on ancient Egypt. Primary sources include archaeological evidence, hieroglyphic texts, tomb inscriptions, and ancient papyri that have been translated and studied by Egyptologists for over two centuries.

Modern scholarly works consulted include publications from leading Egyptologists and institutions such as the British Museum, the Metropolitan Museum of Art, the Egyptian Museum in Cairo, and peer-reviewed academic journals in the field of Egyptology.

Key areas of ongoing scholarly debate—such as precise pyramid construction methods, the extent of certain pharaohs' reigns, and interpretations of religious practices—are presented as the current consensus among historians and archaeologists, with acknowledgment that new discoveries continue to refine our understanding of this ancient civilization.

For young readers interested in learning more, a curated list of age-appropriate resources, including museum websites, educational documentaries, and recommended books, appears in the Resources section at the back of this book.

Every effort has been made to ensure historical accuracy while presenting information in an accessible and engaging manner appropriate for readers ages 8-12.

Index

www.ingramcontent.com/pod-product-compliance
Lightning Source LLC
Chambersburg PA
CBHW050035040726
47599CB00015B/1682